THE WEAPONS ENCYCLOPÆDIA

TANK AIRCRAFT AFV SHIP ARTILLERY VEHICLES SECRET WEAPON

 MESSERSCHMITT BF 109

THE WEAPONS ENCYCLOPAEDIA

EDITORIAL STAFF

Luca Cristini, Paolo Crippa.

CONTRIBUTORS

Enrico Acerbi, Massimiliano Afiero, Aldo Antonicelli, Ruggero Calò, Luigi Carretta, Flavio Chistè, Anna Cristini, Carlo Cucut, Salvo Fagone, Enrico Finazzer, Arturo Giusti, Björn Huber, Andrea Lombardi, Aymeric Lopez, Marco Lucchetti, Luigi Manes, Giovanni Maressi, Francesco Mattesini, Péter Mujzer, Federico Peirani, Alberto Peruffo, Maurizio Raggi, Andrea Alberto Tallillo, Antonio Tallillo, Massimo Zorza.

PUBLISHED BY

Luca Cristini Editore (Soldiershop), via Orio, 35/4 - 24050 Zanica (BG) ITALY.

DISTRIBUTED BY

Soldiershop - www.soldiershop.com, Amazon, Ingram Spark, Berliner Zinnfigurem (D), LaFeltrinelli, Mondadori, Libera Editorial (Spain), Google book (eBook), Kobo, (eBoook), Apple Book (eBook).

ACKNOWLEDGEMENTS

Main contributors to this issue: Björn Huber, author of the profiles, and Luca Cristini. Special thanks to institutions such as: Army General Staff, State Archives, Bundesarchiv, Nara, Library of Congress etc. To the P.Crippa, A.Lopez, L.Manes, C.Cucut, Tallillo archives. Model Victoria (www.modelvictoria.it). The photos were recoloured by Anna Cristini.

For a complete list of Soldiershop titles, or for every information please contact us on our website: www.soldiershop.com or www.cristinieditore.com. E-mail: info@soldiershop.com. Keep up to date on Facebook & Twitter: https://www.facebook.com/soldiershop.publishing

Title: **MESSERSCHMITT BF 109 VOL. 1** Code.: **TWE-018 EN** Series by L. S. Cristini
ISBN code: 9791255890188. First edition December 2023.

THE WEAPONS ENCYCLOPAEDIA (SOLDIERSHOP) is a trademark of Luca Cristini Editore

THE WEAPONS ENCYCLOPÆDIA

TANK AIRCRAFT AFV SHIP ARTILLERY VEHICLES SECRET WEAPON

MESSERSCHMITT BF 109

VOL.1 SERIE A-B-C-D-E

LUCA STEFANO CRISTINI - BJÖRN HUBER

BOOK SERIES FOR MODELERS & COLLECTORS

CONTENTS

▼ Luftwaffe pilots and airmen belonging to the glorious Jagdgeschwader 53 (53rd Fighter Wing) pausing during maintenance work on a Messerschmitt Bf 109 E at a French airport in 1940. In the background can be seen a three-engined Junkers Ju 52. Bundesrchiv licence free.

INTRODUCTION

The Messerschmitt Bf 109 was a single-engine, low-wing monoplane fighter aircraft designed in the 1930s by engineer Willy Messerschmitt, for the German aeronautical company Bayerische Flugzeugwerke AG and produced, as well as by itself and its successor Messerschmitt AG, also under licence in some of its variants by the Romanian Industria Aeronautică Română (IAR) and the Spanish Hispano Aviación, which marketed it as the Hispano Aviación HA-1109. The model is one -maybe the best known- of the German World War II fighters and one of the largest number of combat aircraft built in history (over 33,000 from 1936 to 1945), serving between 1937 and 1947. Until 1941 it was practically the Luftwaffe's only fighter aircraft, after which it was increasingly joined by the Focke-Wulf Fw 190 (see TWE-002). Originally conceived as an interceptor, it proved to be adaptable and versatile enough to be used in numerous roles: fighter-bomber, night fighter, reconnaissance fighter, fighter aircraft, etc. Its structure was designed to easily adapt to continuous upgrades and improvements and the aircraft was still competitive in 1945, more than 10 years after its design in an era of continuous aeronautical progress. It was so successful that numerous variants were produced, so many that it could be said that the first BF-109 and the last, were actually two completely different aircraft!

This is the first of two volumes in which we will discuss this fantastic aircraft, due to the complexity of the weapon. Here I would like to thank the tireless and professional work of my friend Björn Huber, the outstanding author of the beautiful plates and profiles of the aircraft, without whose contribution this work would hardly have been possible.

It was the aircraft most frequently used by the greatest world aviation aces of all time, from Erich Hartmann (the most successful fighter pilot in history, with a *palmares* of over 352 aircraft

▲ Official review of the Luftwaffe's 'Richthofen' fighter wing in August 1938, with General-leutnant Hans-Jürgen Stumpff accompanying French General Vuillemin. The aircraft are all Bf 109 Bs, with the national insignia in use until 1939. See table X. Bundesrchiv free licence.

shot down) to Hans-Joachim Marseille, another great German ace, especially in the African skies. It was also used by other air forces, such as the Finnish, Hungarian, Romanian, Croatian and Italian (RSI) air forces. It was the pride of the Jagdgeschwader 52 (JG 52), the most victorious air force in aviation history.

The abbreviation **Bf,** assigned to the aircraft, indicated the company name of the original company responsible for the design, development and production of the first examples, *Bayerische Flugzeugwerke*, which was renamed *Messerschmitt AG* in July 1938. Models designed from then on assumed the name **Me**, while those designed earlier (including variants, see also the Messerschmitt Bf 110) continued to officially adopt the prefix **Bf**.

◼ DEVELOPMENT AND HISTORY

In early 1934, Germany, as part of the reorganisation of its military air force (the Luftwaffe) with the use of new technology aircraft - the Reichsluftfahrtministerium (RLM), the ministry responsible for aviation in Hitler's Germany - decided to hold a competition for a new high-performance fighter aircraft. This aircraft was to outperform its equivalents in service with the European air forces, simultaneously replacing the Arado Ar 68 and Heinkel He 51 biplanes, which were now considered obsolete. The specifications for the new model, in accordance with earlier discussions by the RLM's Technisches Amt ('Technical Office') in the previous year, called for an all-metal structure with a monoplane wing configuration and retractable landing gear.

In addition, the vehicle was to be equipped with the new, liquid-cooled, 12-cylinder, inverted-V, Junkers Jumo 210 engine, capable of reaching the discrete speed for the time of 400 km/h at an altitude of 6000 m. It was also to reach the aforementioned elevation in 17 minutes and a tangency of 10000 m. The aircraft was to be armed with two 7.92 mm machine guns positioned in the engine bonnet and preferably also a 20 mm cannon integrated in the V of the engine cylinders, following the design solution popular in the 1930s and also adopted by French models. The RLM also required a wing loading of no more than 100 kg/m². Since, given the technology of the time, this performance was not particularly difficult to achieve, the competition attracted the attention of the leading German aircraft companies of the time: Heinkel, Arado and Bayerische Flugzeugwerke. The construction of the prototypes required to enter the competition was three for each competing company, and they had to be completed by the end of 1934. After the prototypes were completed, the one from Bayerische Flugzeugwerke won and was designed by Engineer Willy Messerschmitt, owner and chief designer of a company in Augsburg that worked for the BF. The aircraft was given an operational evaluation during the Spanish Civil War. An initial group of 22 prototypes, derived from further Bf 109 prototypes (V3 and V4) with the designation A-0, was ordered from the RLM. Part of these aircraft was subsequently sent to Spain, assigned to the Condor Legion in early 1937 for operational evaluation in the context of the ongoing conflict. The 'Spanish' aircraft were assigned the tactical designations 6-1 to 6-16 and retained all the features of the original design, including the 600hp Jumo 210 C engine, two MG 17 machine guns and a two-bladed wooden fixed-pitch propeller. However, in the process, numerous minor modifications were made, including the machine gun air intakes and the positioning of the oil cooler. At least one is known to have landed mistakenly behind Republican lines on 11 November 1937 and was subsequently sent to the Soviet Union for examination.

▲ Profile of the Messerschmitt BF 109 first prototype V-1. Work by Björn Huber, licensed under CC BY-SA 3.0.

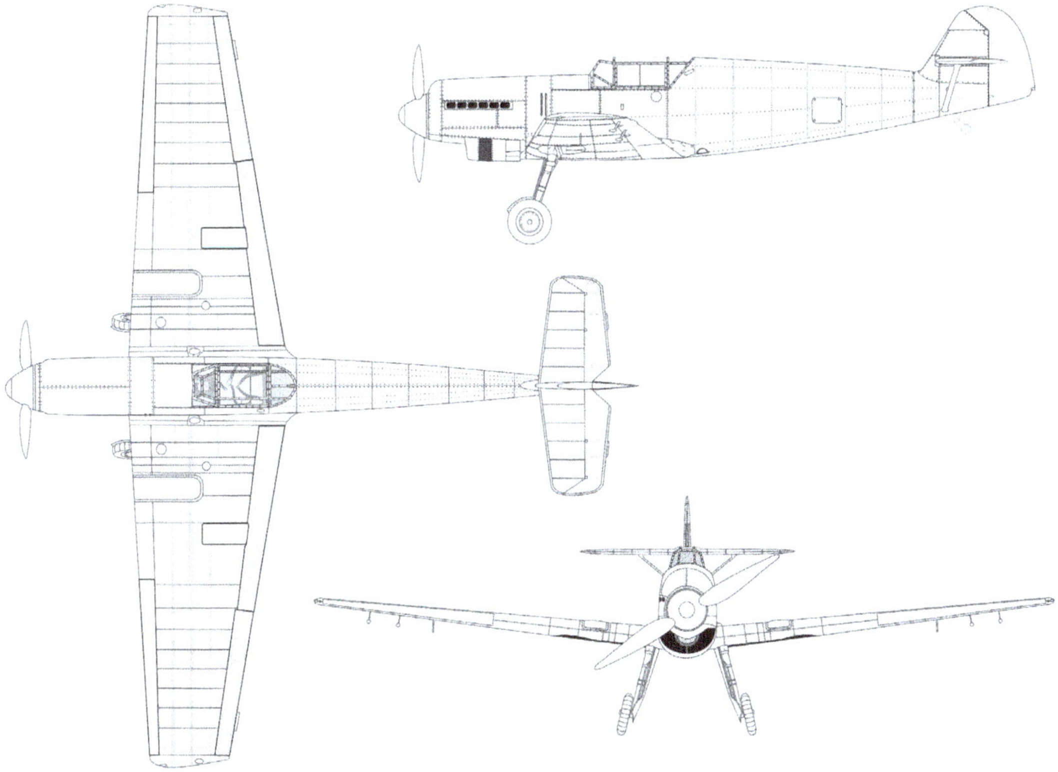

▲ Diagram of the Messerschmitt BF 109 prototype V-1. Work by Björn Huber, licensed under CC BY-SA 3.0.

▲ Luftwaffe ground crew engaged in reloading a Bf 109E, 1939. The 'cat', the emblem of the 2./JG 20 Bundesarchiv, stands out on the aircraft's engine cowling. Author's colouring.

OPERATIONAL CAMPAIGNS

◼ IN THE SKIES OF SPAIN

The first examples of the Bf 109B-1 were delivered to the Luftwaffe's elite unit, the JG 132 'Richthofen', as early as early 1937. Like many other German aircraft models, these aircraft were used in Spain during the Civil War where they had their baptism of fire, framed within the Legion Condor, to replace Heinkel He 51 biplanes. Although they proved highly effective on the ground, the German propaganda ministry chose, for reasons of political expediency, not to publicise the Luftwaffe's involvement in the conflict too much. The first eighteen B-1s and six B-2s were therefore assigned to the 1st and 2nd squadrons of Jagdgruppe 88 (88th Fighter Group), used mainly to counter Republican Polikarpov I-15s and I-16s. In May 1938, two Bf 109C-1s joined the 2nd squadron, and in mid-August the new aircraft equipped the entire 3rd squadron. Among the pilots who particularly distinguished themselves at the controls of the Bf 109 were Werner Mölders (14 victories), Reinhard Seiler (9), Walter Oesau (8), Herbert Ihlefeld (7) and Günther Lützow (5).

Subsequent Bf 109E-1s entered the Spanish front in March 1939, but arrived too late to significantly affect the conflict. One example of this model, with serial number (W.Nr.) 790, was left to the Franco forces and later reacquired in 1960 by the Deutsches Museum. This example is displayed today with the insignia of Jagdgeschwader 26.

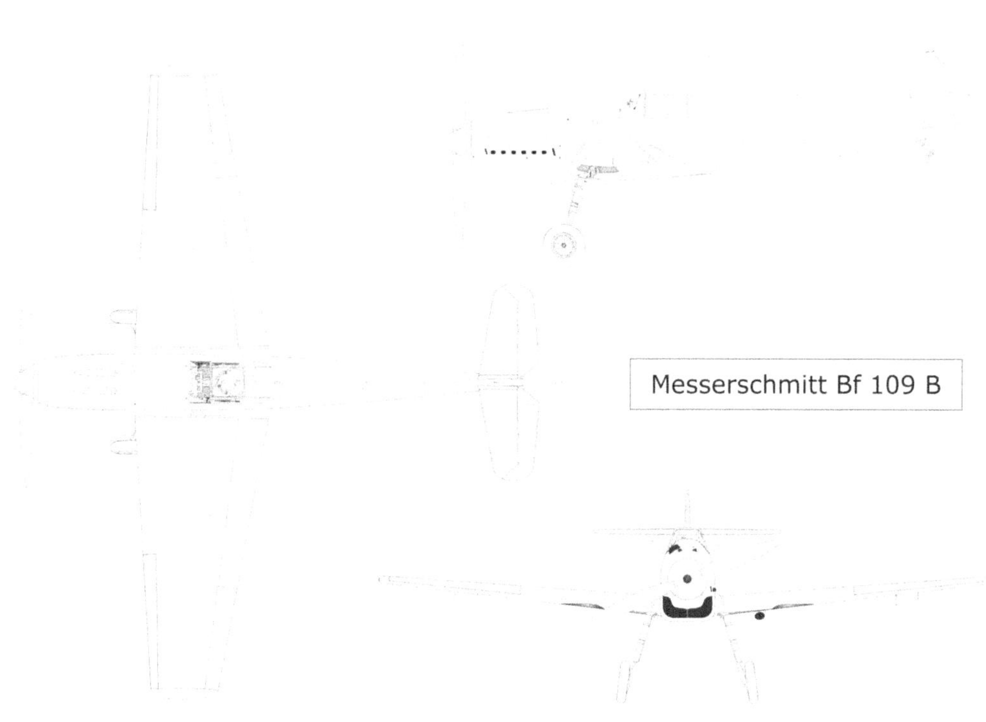

▲ Diagram of the Messerschmitt BF 109 B. Work by Björn Huber, licensed under CC BY-SA 3.0.

▲ Spanish War: Bf 109 C-1 Stab/Jagdgruppe 88, Condor Legion, La Cenia, Spain 1938, Björn Huber.

◼ STORM OVER POLAND

The Bf 109's first official combat mission began with the attack on Poland on 1 September 1939, as part of the Luftwaffe's direct deployment. In the northern region, Air Fleet 1, led by General Albert Kesselring, was ready to support Army Group North, while in the area of Army Group South, General Alexander Löhr's Air Fleet 4 South-East was equally operational. According to reports from the air units, both air fleets had a total of 1,581 aircraft of various types available for operations, compared to only 852 Polish aircraft. The eight fighter groups of the two fleets could count on 342 Bf 109s, 320 of which were declared available and ready for action. To these were also added a further 103 Bf 110 B/Cs (I./ZG 1, I./ZG 76, I.(Z)/LG 1) and 45 Avia B.534 from the Slovakian fighter group ("JGr. Spisska Nova Ves" - 14 machines, "JGr. Piestany" - 31 machines). On the German side, the Bf 109 units deployed included: I./JG 1 (48 Bf 109 E), I./JG 21 (28 Bf 109 D), II. (J)/186 (T) (24 Bf 109 B), II./ZG 1 (39 Bf 109 E), 1./JG 2 (12 Bf 109 E. Finally, the aircraft that only went into action from 10 to 13 September 1939) were: I. (J)/LG 2 (36 Bf 109 E), Stab/LG 2 (3 Bf 109 E), I./ZG 2 (43 Bf 109 D), I./JG 76 (45 Bf 109 E), I. /JG 77 (36 Bf 109 E).

The Polish counterpart fielded 315 PZL P.7 and P.11 fighter planes, characterised by reinforced shoulder wings, fixed landing gear and an open cockpit. Despite their remarkable manoeuvrability, these aircraft achieved absolutely insufficient speeds during flight. Despite the fierce air battles in Poland, with Polish pilots managing to shoot down more than 100 German aircraft in the first six days with the loss of 79 of their planes, most of the Bf 109s shot down over Poland were due to anti-aircraft fire placed on the ground. The often quoted number of 67 Bf 109s shot down over Poland is based on a compilation by the Quartermaster General of the Ob. D. L. and covers the period from 1 to 28 September 1939. However, this figure is not consistent with the available reports of losses, which indicate 32 Bf 109s lost, of which 19 were completely destroyed. The aerial battles showed that the high speed of the Bf 109 and the remarkable manoeuvrability of the P.7 and P.11 forced the German pilots to adopt evasive tactics, avoiding classic corner combat. The Bf-109 pilots preferred to fly their fighters at high speed, approaching from high positions. This strategy would later become the prevalent method of shooting down enemies during the course of the war. After the first week of fighting, the fighter squadrons achieved clear air superiority in Poland, and during this phase, the Bf 109s were increasingly used for close air support with airborne weapons.

MESSERSCHMITT BF 109 A JV88

▲ Messerschmitt - Bf 109 A of the JV 88 (Jagdverband 88), Condor Legion, Spain 1936. Originally built as a V4 prototype of the Bf 109, this aircraft became part of the series of pre-production Bf 109 A aircraft sent to Spain to be tested under combat conditions. Artwork by Björn Huber.

MESSERSCHMITT BF 109 DIFFERENCES BETWEEN VERSION A AND B

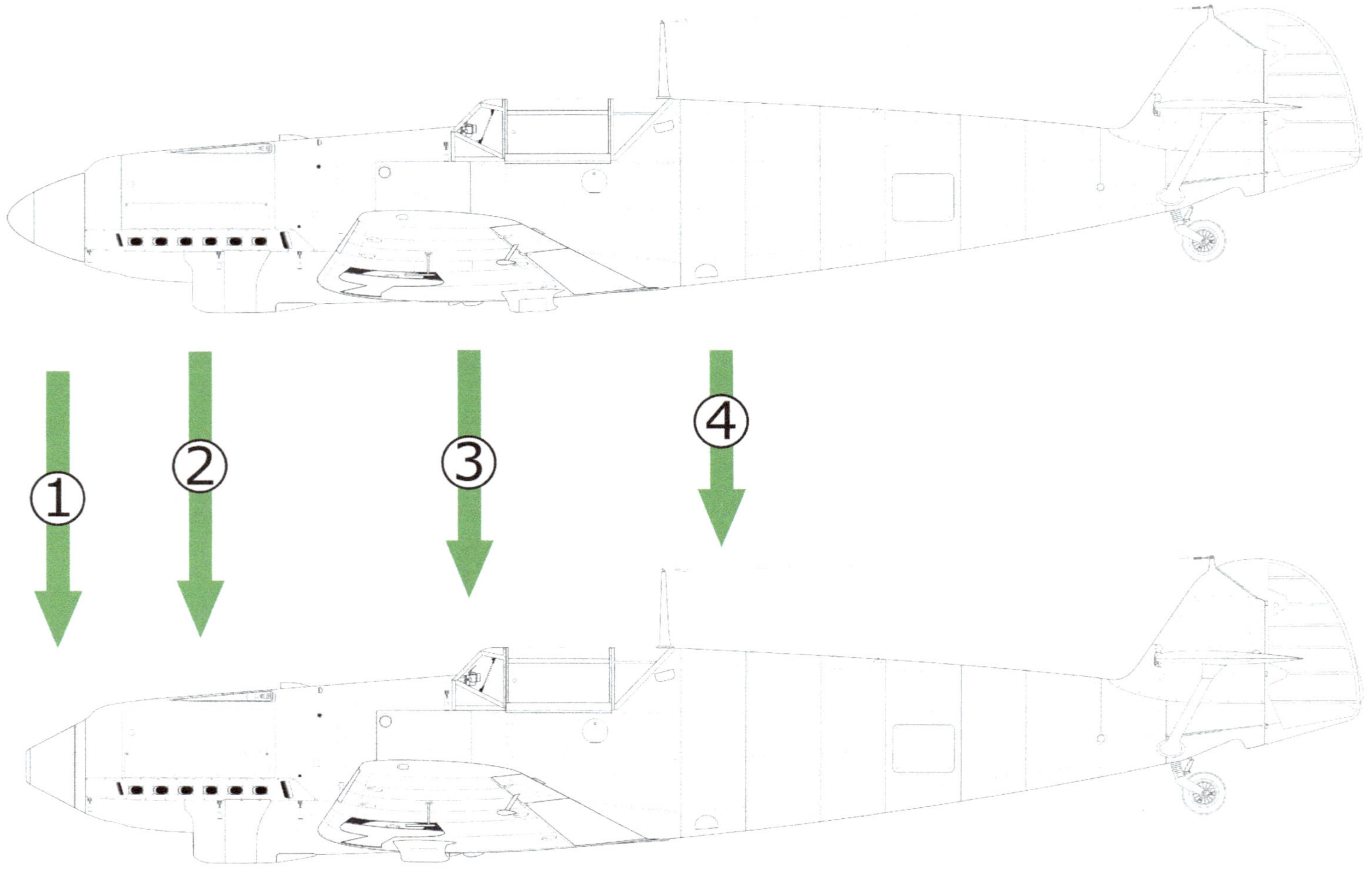

▲ Selected differences between BF 109 A and B: 1. Fixed propeller replaced by variable pitch propeller (the Bf 109 A was set up from the start to use both fixed and variable pitch propellers) 2. For early A version aircraft: flush exhaust doors replaced by slightly raised exhaust doors. 3. Oil cooler under the left wing moved forward towards the engine 4. Deletion of the Elvemag 5 CX bomb loader. Profiles by Björn Huber, licensed under CC BY-SA 3.0.

On French soil, the Luftwaffe's Bf 109 came up against a host of modern fighter planes of the Armée de l'air, such as the Dewoitine D.520, whose air agility was comparable to the famous Bf 109. However, France, with limited financial resources and a defence policy that favoured other military branches, had neglected the development of powerful aircraft in the inter-war period. Competitive models such as the Dewoitine D.520 were therefore only available in limited quantities. Numbers and performance of French fighter units were often overshadowed by aircraft such as the Morane-Saulnier MS.406, a poor aircraft that struggled to hold its own against German fighters. Even the Hawker Hurricane squadrons sent by Britain to support France provided only modest help, as they were mainly older Mk.I versions with 1030 HP (instead of 1300) and fixed propellers. In total, the RAF lost as many as 509 aircraft of various types during operations in France.

Furthermore, the British and French pilots had a whole series of disadvantages not only of a technical but also of an organisational nature. The defence of the French fighters was characterised by absurd and complicated communication channels and unclear command relationships, with overlapping competencies between officers. The rapid advance of the Wehrmacht forced British and French air units to lose one airfield after another, often abandoning unsuitable material or aircraft during their precipitous transfers. The scarcity of usable resources became more and more apparent, with even fuel and ammunition supply problems due to the chaotic conditions. A further disadvantage that contributed to the Luftwaffe's good performance compared to its French and British opponents was the Germanic adoption of more modern tactics, previously developed and tested during the clashes in Spain and Poland. The German formations, organised in swarms (four aircraft), consisting of two squadrons of two machines covering each other, were smaller, more flexible and more agile than their heavy French and British counterparts. Over France, the Bf 109 pilots were able to make the most of their aircraft's characteristics, especially since the main weakness, the short range, was not decisive here. The Luftwaffe's efficient ground organisation allowed the squadrons to quickly take control of newly conquered airfields, reducing distances for the fighter pilots and increasing both reactivity and flight time in operational areas.

THE BATTLE OF ENGLAND

For a time, after the rapid defeat of France, Hitler considered the invasion of the south coast of England (Operation Sea Lion). This plan, known as Operation Sea Lion, was characterised from the outset by inadequate coordination between the German army, navy and air force. Admiral Erich Raeder, commander-in-chief of the Kriegsmarine, considered an amphibious landing on Britain with the few surface units (destroyers) left after the Norwegian campaign to be absolutely impractical and impossible. On its own account, the army did not make serious preparations for an invasion until the essential conditions for a successful operation were in place. Because of the general conditions for an amphibious landing and the superiority of the Royal Navy at sea, the main effort in the preparatory phase of Operation Sea Lion therefore ended up in the hands of the Luftwaffe.

Their first mission was to achieve air superiority over the British Isles and the English Channel and render the British Fighter Command and Bomber Command, which might otherwise have seriously disrupted an amphibious landing, almost harmless. For the effective landing of ground troops it would have been necessary to seal off the Channel to the east and west for at least a few hours. Given the overwhelming naval superiority of the Royal Navy, such a feat would only have been possible through massive air support, the basis of which was itself great air superiority.

After the battles over France, which were disastrous for the British, the RAF took advantage of the phase of relative calm from late June to late July 1940 to reorganise and re-equip Fighter Command. In a realistic assessment of the situation, its commander-in-chief, Air Chief Marshal Sir Hugh Dowding, had retained the most valuable (because most powerful) Supermarine Spitfire fighters to protect the soil and skies of the British homeland. Thanks to the efforts of the minister responsible for aircraft construction, Lord Beaverbrook, and the influx of trained pilots from France and throughout the Commonwealth, Dowding was able to supply 609 single-seat Hawker Hurricane and Supermarine Spitfire fighters at the start of the Battle of Britain. The exact date of the start of the Battle of Britain is not easy to determine. On 20 July, the day after Hitler gave a speech to Britain in which he attempted to heavily intimidate the British government, the number of Bf 109s in the Luftwaffe's fighter squadrons returned to 809 aircraft after making up for losses in the French campaign.

At that time, also because of the terrible weather in the summer of 1940, only sporadic air battles took place between British and German fighters engaged in a kind of 'free fighter'. It was only when the Luftwaffe was ordered to seal the Channel that the first major air battles began. During this phase, British pilots still continued to use obsolete tactics and suffered heavy losses. As a result, the Luftwaffe's closure of the channel to British maritime traffic was successful.

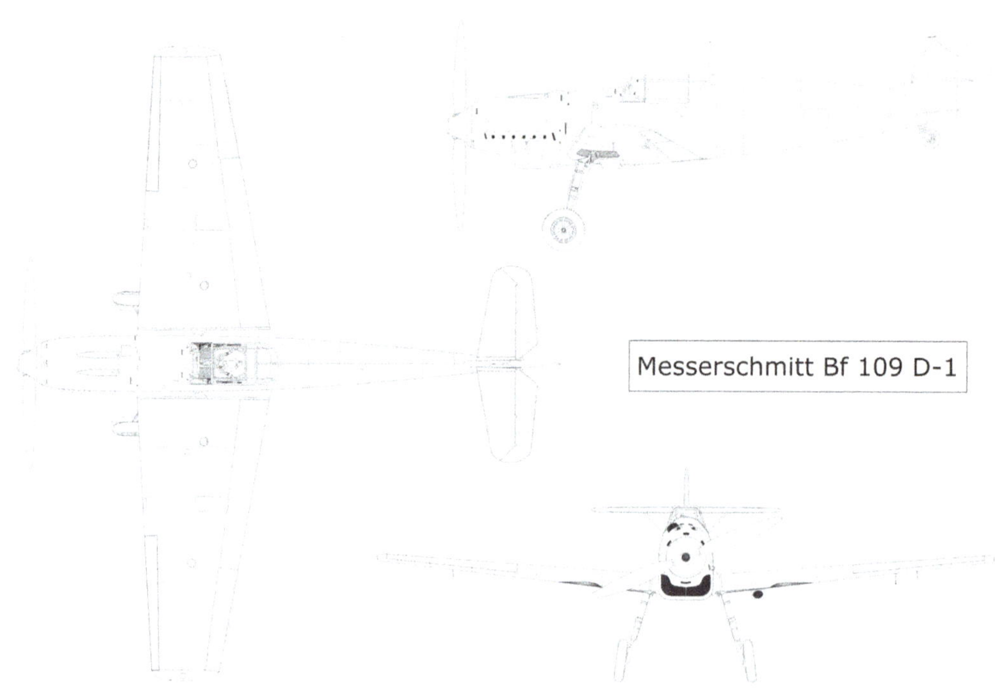

▲ Diagram of the Messerschmitt BF 109 D1. Work by Björn Huber, licensed under CC BY-SA 3.0.

MESSERSCHMITT BF 109 A DIFFERENCES BETWEEN B AND C VERSIONS

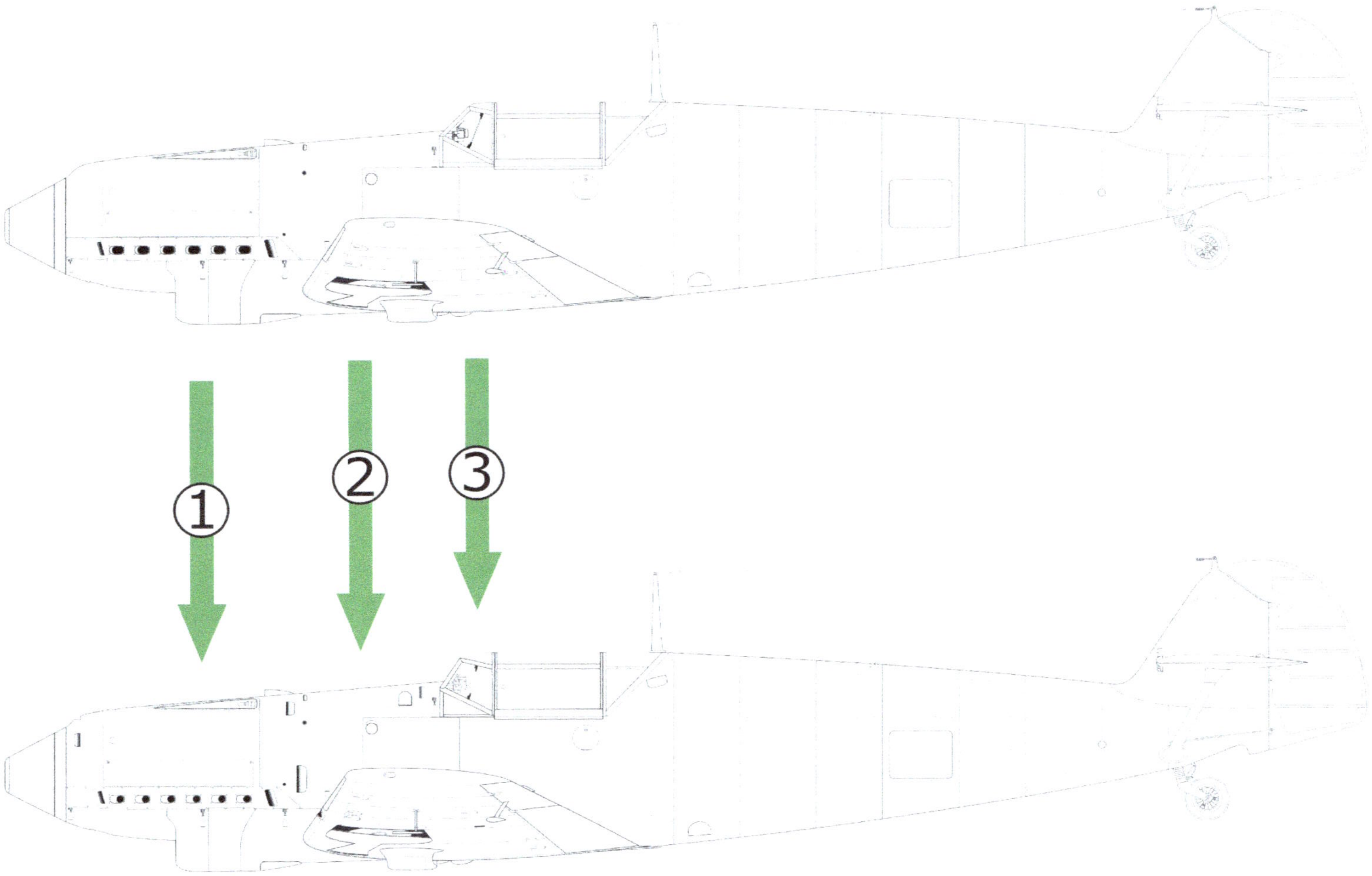

▲ Selected differences between BF 109 B and C: 1. Junkers Jumo 210D engine replaced by Jumo 210G with fuel injection. 2. Addition of a 7.92 mm MG 17 in each wing (1000 rounds per weapon). 3. Revi C12/C sight replaced by Revi C12/D. Profiles by Björn Huber.

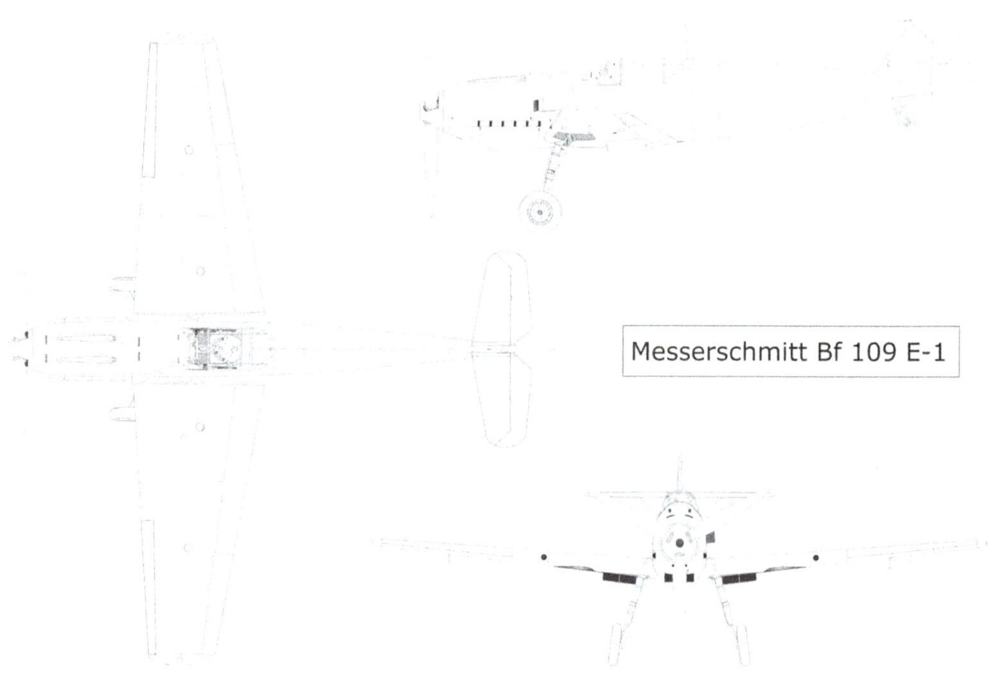

▲ Battle of Britain: British soldiers beside a Messerschmitt bf 109e-4 of 6./jg 51 'Molders', forced to crash-land at East Langdon in Kent, 24 August 1940. The pilot, Oberfeldwebel Beeck, was captured unhurt.

▲ Diagram of the Messerschmitt BF 109 E1. Work by Björn Huber, licensed under CC BY-SA 3.0.

MESSERSCHMITT BF 109 B JG 132 RICHTHOFEN

▲ Messerschmitt - Bf 109 B of II./JG 132 (Jagdgeschwader 132) 'Richthofen' at Jüterbog-Damm, spring 1937 - one of the first 109s assigned to a Luftwaffe unit in Germany. Artwork by Björn Huber.

MESSERSCHMITT BF 109 A DIFFERENCES BETWEEN C AND D VERSIONS

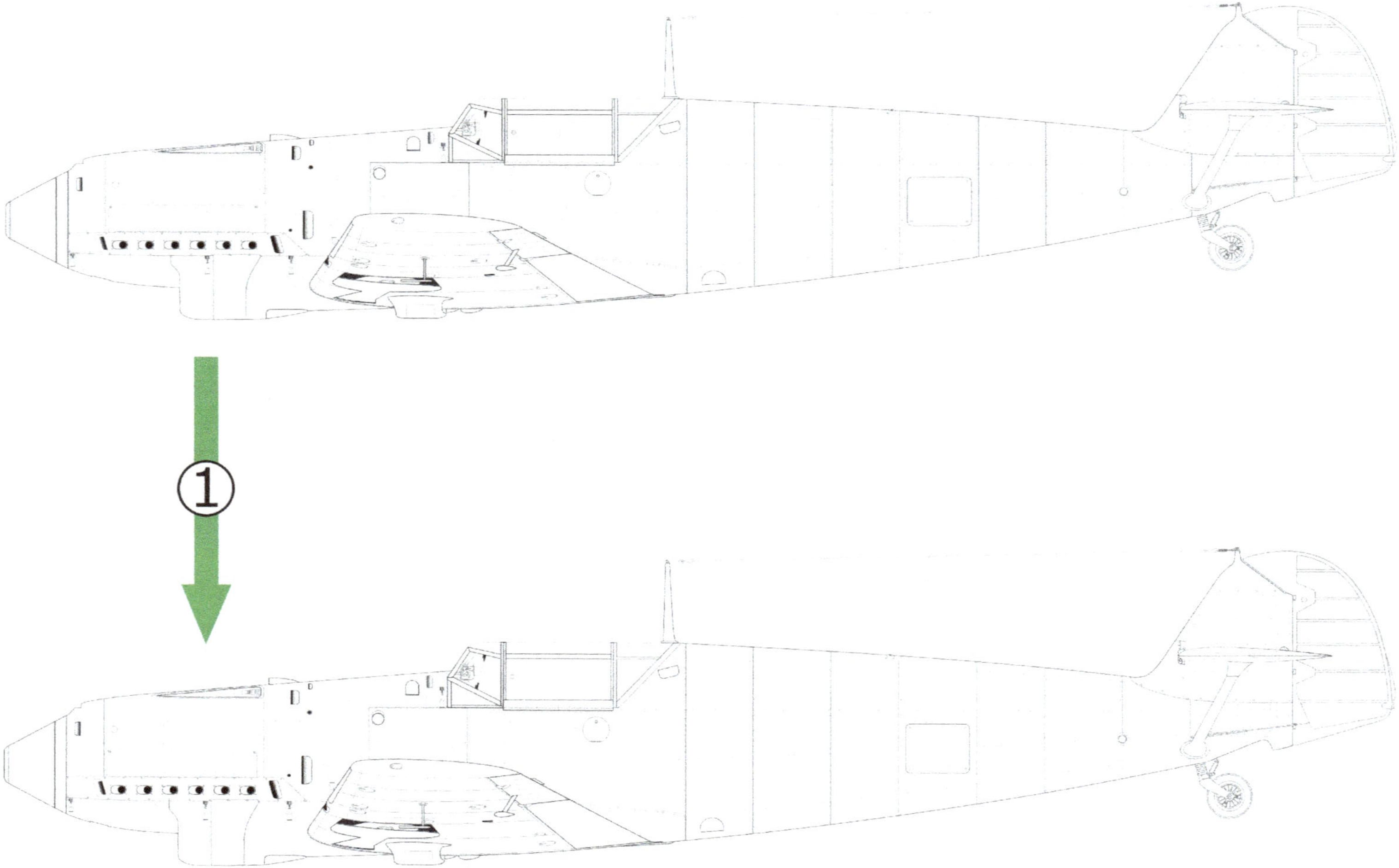

▲ Selected differences between BF 109 C and D: 1. Junkers Jumo 210G engine with fuel injection replaced by Jumo 210D due to lack of Jumo 210G. Profiles by Björn Huber, released under licence CC BY-SA 3.0.

▲ The tail of a BF-109 at an airfield in the Balkans, with all trophies and victories won neatly depicted on the tail of the aircraft. Bundesarchiv. Author colouring.

▼ France: four Messerschmitt BF 109 E fighter planes of the 51 Mölders (IV. JG 51) fighter squadron at the field airfield; PK 670, Bundesarchiv. Author colouring.

MESSERSCHMITT BF 109 A DIFFERENCES BETWEEN D AND E VERSION

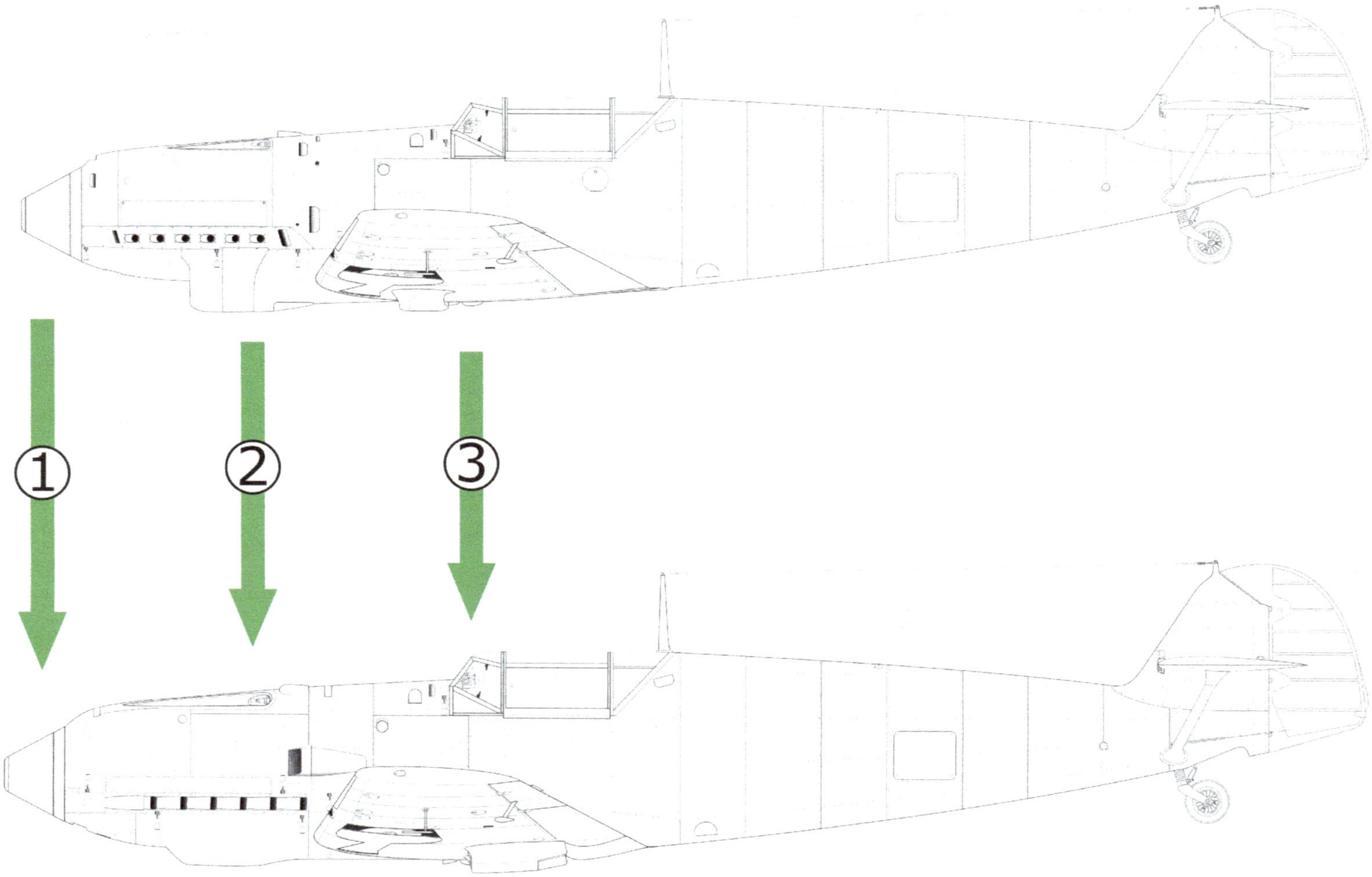

▲ Selected differences between BF 109 D and E: 1. Replacement of the two-blade variable-pitch propeller with a three-blade variable-pitch propeller. 2. Replacement of the Jumo 210D engine with a Daimler Benz DB 601 A engine. 3. Rebuilding of the engine cowling with relocation of the oil cooler under the engine and two water coolers under the wings. Profiles by Björn Huber, licensed under CC BY-SA 3.0.

AIR WAR IN NORTH AFRICA

On 11 February 1941, the first Wehrmacht troops stepped onto African soil with the aim of aiding the besieged Italian forces in North Africa from the relentless British advance in Operation Sunflower. The German Afrika Korps (DAK), under the command of Erwin Rommel, flanked the units of III./ZG 26, LG 1, StG 1 and StG 2, supported by three reconnaissance squadrons. In particular, ZG 26 played a key role in pressing the retreating British units towards Tobruk. On 18 April 1941, the first Bf 109 E of 1./JG 27 touched down at Ain el Gazala airfield. Other squadrons of 1./JG 27, with Ensign Hans-Joachim Marseille among the protagonists, and 7./JG 26 became active immediately. In addition to interception, the Bf 109 E's had the main task of providing tactical support to army units, including the delicate task of protecting vulnerable Ju 87s. In September 1941, the first squadrons returned to Germany to switch to Bf 109 Fs before being redeployed to the African theatre. Facing aircraft such as the Tomahawk and Kittyhawk, along with the ubiquitous Hurricanes, the Bf 109 had to cope with several challenges. The Tomahawk, with its low maximum altitude of 9,140 metres, and the Hurricane, with a carburettor engine, proved to be less effective than the Bf 109 F, which flew at a maximum altitude of over 10,660 metres and boasted a higher speed of about 60 km/h. During ground battles, the British 8th Army launched a counter-offensive in November 1941, forcing Rommel to break the siege of Tobruk and withdraw. The failure to capture Malta proved to be a serious mistake, leading to a withdrawal of parts of Air Fleet 2 from the Soviet Union to reinforce Africa, including the entire JG 53 and II./JG 3. On 21 January 1942, the DAK offensive kicked off, pushing back British troops in late February and capturing Cyrenaica. While the DAK continued its attack on El Alamein on 1 July, the Bf 109 was employed in numerous individual battles against RAF combat units. At the end of July 1942, the North African front stabilised, shifting the battle back to Malta.

▲ Throughout the conflict, the Luftwaffe was a master of aircraft camouflage: these Bf 109E of I. Gruppe JG 27 in flight over Libya are an excellent example. The picture is from spring 1941.

MESSERSCHMITT BF 109 C JG 71

▲ Messerschmitt - Bf 109 C of 2./JG 71 (Jagdgeschwader 71), summer 1939; the aircraft had a shark's mouth painted on it for propaganda reasons.
Artwork by Björn Huber.

MESSERSCHMITT BF 109 D JV 88 HOLZAUGE

▲ Messerschmitt - Bf 109 D of JV 88 (Jagdverband 88), Condor Legion, Spain 1938. The sign 'Holzauge' (wooden eye) is a reference to a German saying urging permanent vigilance. Artwork by Björn Huber.

▲ North African Front: pilot of a Messerschmitt Me 109 fighter before deployment; KBK Lw 7. Bundesarchiv.

▼ Several Messerschmitt Bf 109B at Budaörs Airport, 1937. Wiki CC3 by Fortepan/Horváth József Wikipedia, author colour

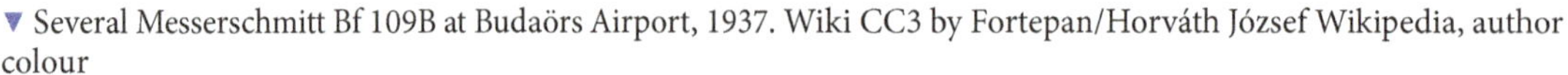

THE VEHICLE'S SERIES

BF 109 V: prototypes (from the German *Versuch)*

The Bf 109 V1 (first prototype) began its first taxi trials in the spring of 1935, followed by its first flight on 28 May 1935 with flight captain Hans-Dietrich Knoetzsch in Augsburg- Haunstetten. The civil registration number of the aircraft was D-IABI. The non-adjustable two-bladed wooden propeller came from the Schwarz company. During comparative flights at Travemünde, the Bf 109 V1 demonstrated a top speed of 470 km/h at an altitude of 3300 metres and a climb rate of 13.7 m/s near the ground with a take-off weight of 1900 kilograms.

The second V2 prototype (serial no. D-IILU, serial no. 759) was already equipped with the Jumo 210 engine later intended for series production. The machine also had all the facilities for the installation of two 7.92 mm MG 17 machine guns, each with 500 rounds of ammunition. After the factory tests, Wurster transferred the V2 to Travemünde on 21 February 1936, where he successfully demonstrated it several times over the following days.

The armament of the two MG 17s already intended for the V2, also equipped with a mechanical through-loading device, was only supplied to the third V3 prototype (D-IOQYopera No. 760), which formed the model aircraft for the planned A-0 series of the Bf 109. When it became clear that modern British fighters would be equipped with eight machine guns, the technical office considered the armament of the Bf 109 A to be inadequate.

With the V3, an attempt was made to significantly increase firepower with a 20 mm MG FF machine gun mounted behind the engine block, the barrel of which passed through the hollow shaft of the propeller. Testing had to be interrupted due to strong vibrations and thermal problems. So the next machine to be completed, the V4 (D-IALY, work no. 878), initially had

▲ Diagram of the Messerschmitt BF 109 E-4. Work by Björn Huber, licensed under CC BY-SA 3.0.

▲ Bf 109 B-1 Nr4 Dübendorf in 1937. Artwork by Herbert Ringlstetter released under CC3 wiki licence.

two machine guns that could be loaded mechanically. However, it was eventually designated as a model aircraft for the now planned B-series of the Bf 109. Only the V5 (D-IIGO, Job No. 879) received three MG 17s, which could now be loaded electromechanically. Again, the third central machine gun was installed behind the engine and fired through the propeller shaft. The V4 was the last 109 tested at Travemünde. With Carl Francke's move to the Rechlin electronics site, all other fighter tests were also moved there.

From December 1936, the V3 and V4 prototypes were initially tested under combat conditions as part of the Jagdgruppe 88, which belonged to the Condor Legion. The new fighter proved technically superior to all other fighters used in the Spanish Civil War, mostly Soviet and Italian aircraft, such as the Polikarpov I-16. During the three years that this conflict lasted, numerous variants of the Bf 109 were used and tested, culminating in the stable E version. In this way, the Luftwaffe acquired a great deal of knowledge about modern air warfare, which was constantly incorporated into both technical and tactical improvements.

While the use of the first Bf 109 in the Spanish Civil War gave experts pause for thought, the advanced aircraft was demonstrated in detail at the 4th International Aviation Congress from 23 July to 1 August 1937 at the Dübendorf military airfield near Zurich. There, six Bf 109s competed against aircraft and pilots from other countries and won all the competitions they took part in. Carl Francke won the climb and dive competition in his V7 (D-IJHA, Opus No. 881), Ernst Udet, then Chief of the Air Force Technical Office and Major General since April 1937, had won in his V14 (D-ISLU, Opus No. 1029). Francke also won at Dübendorf, who was later entered with his V13 (D-IPKY, serial number 1050). Here too, the German Major Hans Seidemann, won in turn, probably aboard the V9 with a Jumo 210 G, which completed the 367 km course in 56 minutes and 47 seconds as the fastest. The same competition in class C, patrols of three, was eventually won by the Bf-109 team with Captain Werner Restemeier, Oblt. Fritz Schleif and oblt. Hannes Trautloft . Finally, the Bf 109 V14 (D-ISLU) was the first prototype of the E-series. It was created in the summer of 1938 A DB-601-A engine served as propulsion. The armament consisted of 2 × 20 mm MG/FF in the wings and 2 × 7.92 mm MG 17 above the engine. The Bf 109 V16 (D-IPGS) was the model aircraft of the E-3 series.

BF 109 A: first series version

The A series corresponded in almost every detail to the later B series; a distinguishing feature recognisable from the outside was the oil cooler on the underside. All 20 machines were produced in Augsburg. Most were sent to Spain for operational testing.

▲ Messerschmitt - Bf 109 D from I./ZG 2 (Zerstörergeschwader 2), Polish campaign, September 1939. Artwork by Björn Huber.

MESSERSCHMITT BF 109 DIFFERENCES BETWEEN VERSION E1 AND E3

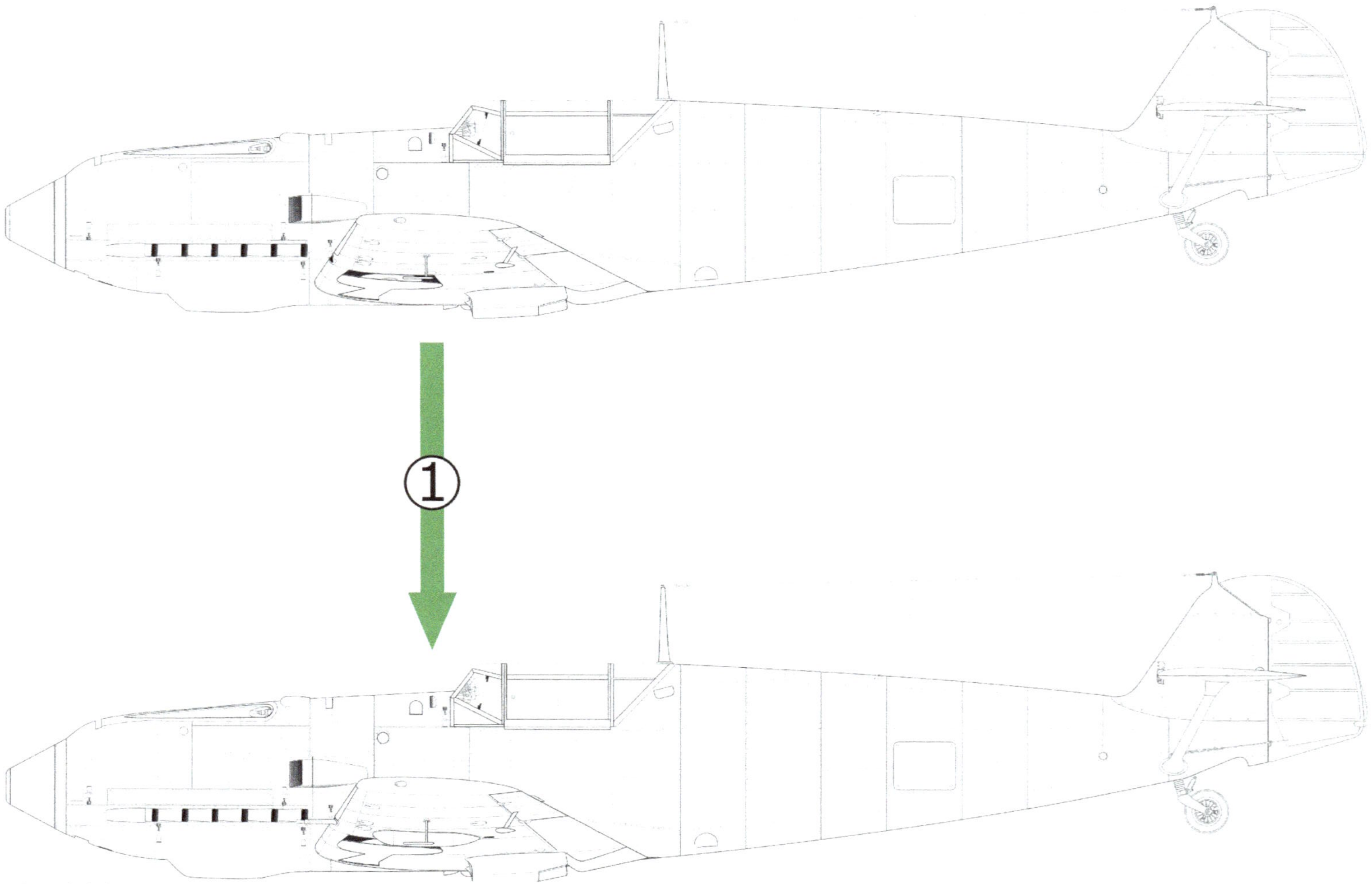

▲ Selected differences between BF 109 E1 and E3: 1. Replacement of the 7.92 mm MG 17 mounted on the wings with a 20 mm MG FF (60 rounds per weapon). Profiles by Björn Huber, licensed under CC BY-SA 3.0.

▲ Western Front: a Messerschmitt Me 109 of the StaffelAbzeichen (Battle Axe) Squadron Bundesarchiv.

BF 109 B:

At the same time that the Bf 109 prototypes were being tested as part of the Legion Condor mission in Spain, the Luftwaffe received its first B-series aircraft. With a take-off weight of around 2200 kg, the Bf 109 B-1 was powered by the 680 hp Junkers Jumo 210 D engine.

Compared to the prototypes, the oil cooler had now been moved out of the large chin radiator cowling and placed under the left side of the wing. As with the V5 prototype, the armament consisted of three MG 17s, which were now aimed with a Zeiss C/12 reflex sight.

The first unit to convert to the new fighter was the JG 132 Richthofen (II./JG 132), stationed at the Jüterbog-Damm airbase. Other examples of the B series, of which around 350 were built, and also around 50 of the C version, were the I./JG 131 in Jesau, the JG 134 'Horst Wessel' in Dortmund, the JG 135 in Bad Aibling, the JG 234 'Schlageter' in Cologne and the II./JG 333 in Eger.

After the construction of some 30 machines, the production line was then converted from the old propeller to the new controllable two-bladed metal propeller (Hamilton Standard licence) from Junkers Flugzeug und Motorenwerke. This version was unofficially called the B-2, but was not mentioned as such in any official documents. Many Bf 109 B-1s were also converted to the new variable-pitch propeller, and a small number of aircraft were said to have been converted to the more powerful Jumo 210 G engine with direct petrol injection, which developed an increased power output of as much as 730 hp at an altitude of 1,000 metres.

The B-series machines were made available to Jagdgruppe 88 of the Condor Legion in Spain for testing under operational conditions. This showed even more of a significant change in performance compared to the prototypes. In contrast, the machine gun, which fired through the hollow shaft of the propeller and was mounted behind the engine block, still proved to be very delicate and susceptible to jamming due to overheating. Based on these experiences, the mid-engine machine guns of the Bf 109 B used in Jagdgruppe 88 were mostly removed in the field workshops and their installation was soon abandoned in series production.

MESSERSCHMITT BF 109 E-1 DEL 2/LG 2

▲ Messerschmitt - Bf 109 E-1 of 2./LG 2 (Lehrgeschwader 2), Polish campaign, September 1939. Artwork by Björn Huber.

MESSERSCHMITT BF 109 DIFFERENCES BETWEEN E3 AND E4 VERSIONS

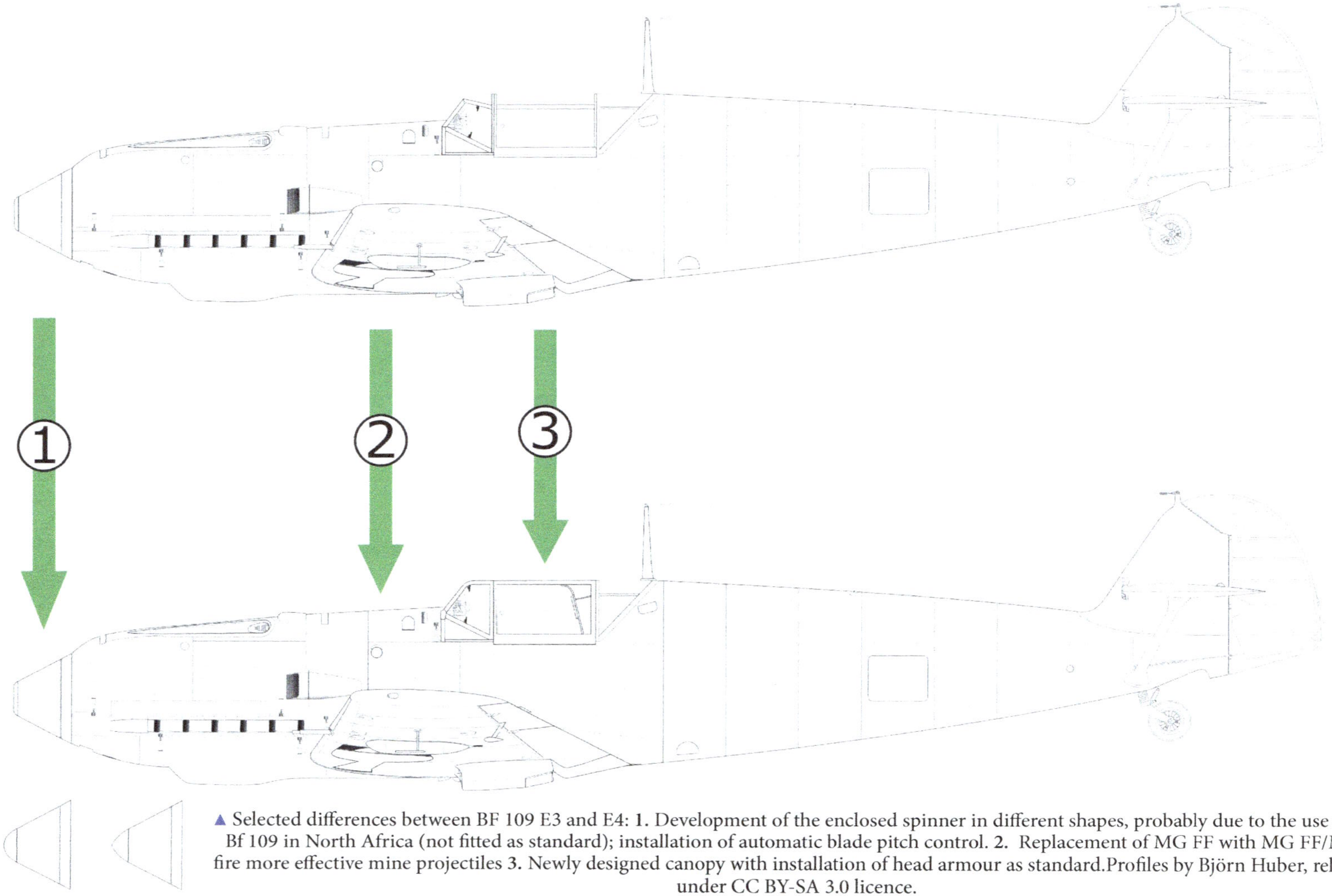

▲ Selected differences between BF 109 E3 and E4: 1. Development of the enclosed spinner in different shapes, probably due to the use of the Bf 109 in North Africa (not fitted as standard); installation of automatic blade pitch control. 2. Replacement of MG FF with MG FF/M to fire more effective mine projectiles 3. Newly designed canopy with installation of head armour as standard.Profiles by Björn Huber, released under CC BY-SA 3.0 licence.

▲ Western Front: a Messerschmitt Bf 109G6R6 JG3 in maintenance.

Main Variants Bf 109 B
- · Bf 109 B-1: fighter; Junkers Jumo 210 D engine with 680 hp starting power, armament initially 3, then 2 × 7.92 mm MG 17;
- · Bf 109 B-2: fighter, unofficial name for Bf 109 B-1 with variable pitch propeller.

■ BF 109 C:

The negative experience with machine guns in Spain and the general desire to increase armament led to the development of the Bf-109-C series. For the first time, two non-synchronised MG 17s were installed on the wings, so that the armament increased to a total of four such machine guns. The first aircraft equipped in this way was the prototype V11 D-IFMO.

The engine used was the Jumo 210 G with direct petrol injection, which had already been used in some B-series aircraft and allowed a top speed of 470 km/h with a starting power of 730 hp at an altitude of 4000 metres. The Jumo 210 G's direct petrol injection also allowed flight manoeuvres to be performed with negative G-forces without engine misfires.

Another improvement on the C Series concerned the engine exhaust system. While the B-Series still had flush exhausts, which imposed a high thermal load on the surrounding structure, the new variant had clearly protruding and slightly backward curved exhaust pipes, which achieved a significant reduction in load and generated additional thrust.

Like its predecessors, the C series was also tested during the Spanish Civil War. The planned further developments were no longer put into series production. With the C-2, a 20-mm MG FF-type central machine gun installed behind the engine was tested again, without success. The attempt to install two MG FFs in the wings, which was tested on the V12 at the Travemünde test site, also had to be abandoned due to problems with the strength of the wing structure.

◼ BF 109 D:

In the original invitation to tender for the 1934 fighter competition, the RLM technical office required the easy interchangeability of the Junkers Jumo 210 with a displacement of 19.7 litres, which at the time was further developed from the considerably more powerful 33.9 litre Daimler Benz DB 600 engine. The D series of the Bf 109 was thus to receive a new engine that had previously been tested in the V11 and V12 prototypes (converted from B and C machines). The first series model, the DB 600 Aa, with a starting power of 960 hp provided a further significant increase in performance. Indeed, it seems doubtful that most of the 600 or so Bf 109 Ds built were actually equipped with the DB-600 engine. This engine also powered the early versions of the He 111, which at the time as a bomber enjoyed high priority in Luftwaffe development. Furthermore, the DB 600 was rated reliable enough for twin-engine aircraft, but not for single-engine aircraft. As Daimler-Benz had already pushed ahead with the development of the even more powerful DB 601 with direct petrol injection, the Bf 109 D-1 series were powered by Jumo 210 engines like their predecessors, so they hardly differed from each other.

Nazi propaganda cleverly concealed this fact by photographing the few machines with DB-600 engines with ever new layers of paint. In fact, there are relatively few photos today that even show a Bf 109 with a DB 600 engine.

◼ BF 109 E:

In January 1939, production of the Bf 109 finally switched to the new E-1 version. After the less reliable DB 600 carburettor engine proved a disappointment, the more powerful DB 601 fuel-injected engine was installed in the E-1, which at the time was one of the most modern aircraft engines in the world. Tested in the V14 and V15 prototypes, the DB 601 A-1, equipped with Bosch direct petrol injection, delivered a starting power of around 990 hp.

From the spring of 1939, the Bf 109 E-1 replaced the old B and C models. The transition to the E version was completed in the autumn of 1939.

On the outside, the 'Emil', as this model was amicably called, featured a completely redesigned engine bonnet. The characteristic previous radiator was considerably reduced in size and now housed only the oil cooler. The two coolers for the glycol-water mixture were housed in flat

MESSERSCHMITT BF 109 E 1 8 JG 26 EDUARD NEUMANN

▲ Messerschmitt - Bf 109 E-1 of 8./JG 26 (Jagdgeschwader 26) flown by Eduard Neumann, autumn 1939. Neumann later became a well-known unit commander of JG 27 in North Africa and was credited with a total of 13 air victories. The emblem depicts Adamson, a comic book character popular in the 1920s, who was painted on all aircraft of the so-called 'Adamson-Staffel' 8./JG 26. Artwork by Björn Huber.

housings under the wings. Overall, this greatly improved the aerodynamic lines which, together with the more powerful engine, led to a sudden increase in performance.

While the E-1 was initially equipped with the same armament as its predecessors (4 × 7.92 mm MG 17), the Bf 109 E-3, which entered service at the end of 1939, finally succeeded in its objective of significantly strengthening the installation of wing-mounted automatic cannons. The attempt to install a central cannon behind the engine had previously failed with the E-2 version. The wing cannons were 20mm MG FF guns, derived from the Swiss 20mm cannon of Maschinenfabrik Oerlikon. The guns fired non-synchronously outside the propeller circle and were stored in a drum magazine with 60 rounds per gun. This equipment was relatively scarce and barely sufficient for about seven seconds of continuous fire. In addition, the cannon, with its short barrel, had worse ballistics than the MG 17 machine guns. These disadvantages were compensated for by the availability of explosive ammunition and, starting with the E-4, highly effective mine ammunition with detonator fuses.

The E series was the first version of the Bf 109, sold on a large scale not only to Luftwaffe fighter units, but also to foreign users. By the winter of 1938/39, Switzerland had already imported ten Bf 109 Ds with Junkers engines and subsequently ordered a total of 30 Bf 109 E-3s. After the arrival of the first machines, the order was increased to 50 machines. Aeroplanes of this type were also sold to Yugoslavia.

Production of the Bf 109 was greatly expanded with the E series and reached a new high with 1,100 machines built in the first eight months of 1939. This variant was also tested in Spain and, by the time World War II began with the German attack on Poland, the Bf 109 E already made up the majority of German fighter units. Of the 320 operational Bf 109s involved in the raid on Poland, as many as 213 came from the E series. Used over Poland, Norway and France, the Bf 109 E proved to be an extremely capable fighter aircraft, flown by well-trained and sometimes combat-experienced pilots. The disadvantage of the short range had little bearing on the Wehrmacht's early campaigns. It was only during the Battle of Britain, when German fighter squadrons first encountered large-scale opponents on a par (both in terms of technology and - with a certain lag - in terms of tactics) that the Bf 109 E's strengths and weaknesses became apparent. Among the pros, at medium and high altitudes the Bf 109 E was faster than the Spitfire and at all altitudes significantly faster than the Hurricane. This height advantage was exploited again and again by German pilots when they were able to pounce on British fighters attacking German bombers from high positions during escort missions. With an armament of two 20 mm MG FF cannons and two 7.92 mm MG 17 machine guns, the BF 109 E also had more firepower than the British fighters with their battery of eight 7.7 mm MGs, mainly due to the explosive ammunition of the automatic cannons.

Compared to the British Spitfire and Hurricane fighters, the Bf 109 E had a larger turning radius. Although it had a higher lift coefficient and weighed less than the Spitfire, it still had a turning radius about 20 per cent larger at the same speed due to its considerably smaller wing. In terms of diving speed, the Bf 109 E outperformed both British models.

Another advantage of the Bf 109 E was the Daimler-Benz engine with direct fuel injection, which made it possible to push it forcefully into a dive without the engine shutting down (a well-known defensive manoeuvre in air combat tactics). The British carburettor-engined aircraft had to start the dive with a time-consuming half-roll and therefore could not follow it fast enough. In contrast, the biggest disadvantage of the Bf 109 E at the time of the Battle of Britain

▲ Luftwaffe 1.NAG2 air crew with its commander, Staffelkaptain or Staka Herbert Garten Uman Cherkasy, Ukraine, February 1944, in the foreground.

▼ Messerschmitt Bf-109 B-Yellow-1-in a Germany airfield 1939

MESSERSCHMITT BF 109 DIFFERENCES BETWEEN E4 AND E7 VERSIONS

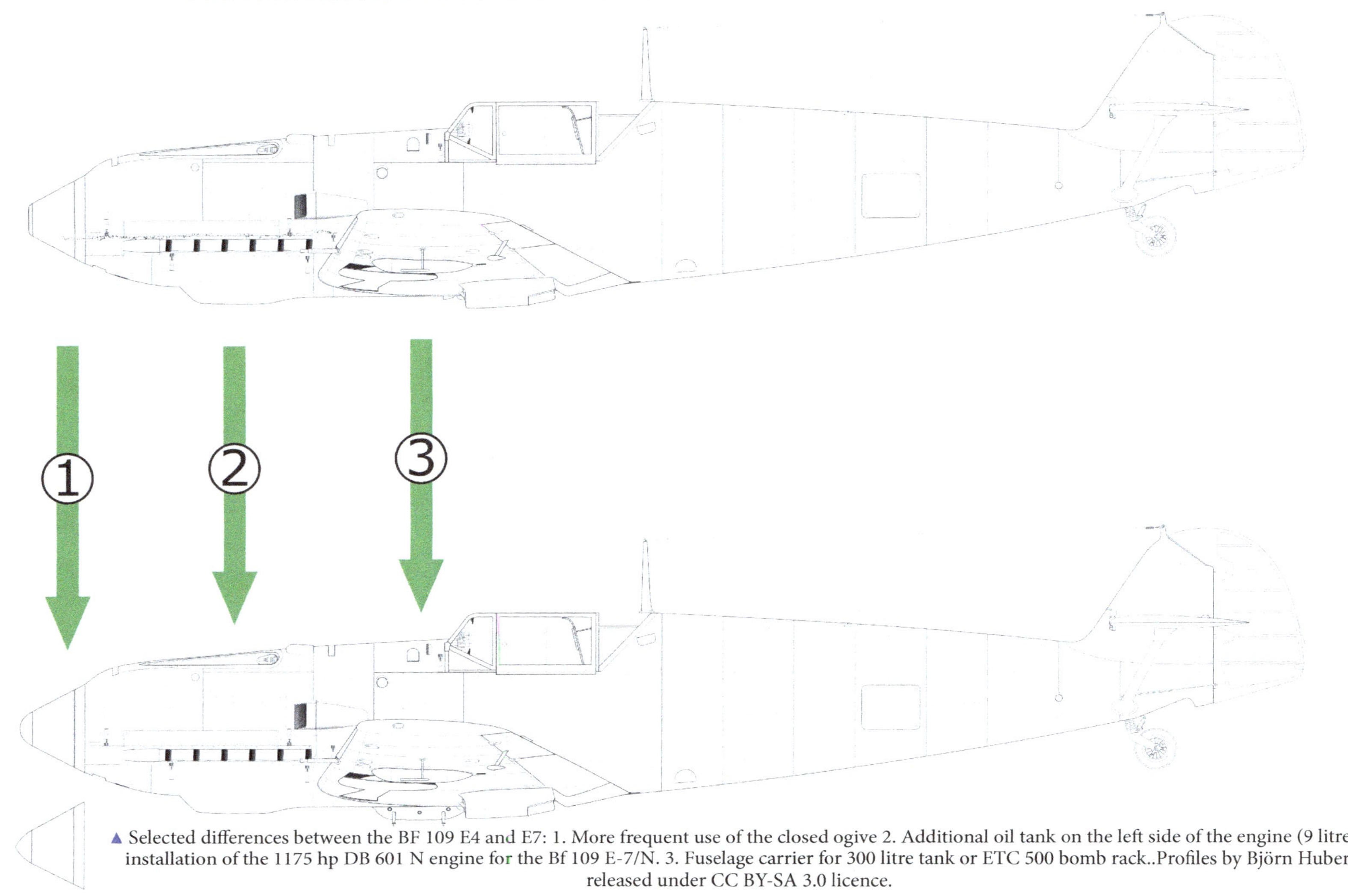

▲ Selected differences between the BF 109 E4 and E7: 1. More frequent use of the closed ogive 2. Additional oil tank on the left side of the engine (9 litres); installation of the 1175 hp DB 601 N engine for the Bf 109 E-7/N. 3. Fuselage carrier for 300 litre tank or ETC 500 bomb rack..Profiles by Björn Huber, released under CC BY-SA 3.0 licence.

▲ Messerschmitt Bf 109E van 4 (S)/LG 2 (Lehrgeschwader 2). Wiki CC3 by Fotoafdrukken Koninklijke Luchtmacht

▼ Mechanic at work maintaining a Messerschmitt Bf 109E4 5th Staffel Black on a French field in 1940. Bundesarchiv, author colour.

MESSERSCHMITT BF 109 E 3 I/ JG 52

▲ Messerschmitt - Bf 109 E-3 from I./JG 52 (Jagdgeschwader 52) French Campaign, Spring 1940. Artwork by Björn Huber.

▲ German airmen during maintenance of the BF-109 cannon, placed in the hollow core of the propeller. Bundesarchiv, author's colours.

▼ France, September 1940: Interesting picture showing the MG17 machine gun synchronisation check of an Me 109E-3. Bundesarchiv, author's colouring.

was its short range or range. During escort missions, German pilots often only had enough fuel on their targets for ten to a maximum of 20 minutes of aerial combat and were often forced to choose between abandoning the bombers or risking a ditching in the English Channel for lack of fuel. Before the start of the air battles over England, the development of the E-series had brought with the E-4 a new, simplified cockpit cowling with improved armour, but the urgently needed introduction of truly adequate armour could not be completed before the end of the Battle of Britain. This only became possible in the autumn of 1940 with the E-7 version.

After the Battle of Britain, the Bf 109 E-series was used in ever new roles. In addition to the E-5 and E-6 reconnaissance variants, the Bf 109 E-4/B was developed as a fighter-bomber with which the fighter squadron could carry out small hit-and-run missions against important targets on the English south coast. This variant was also introduced in some fighter-bomber squadrons, whose Bf 110 aircraft had proved vulnerable to fighter attacks. The Bf 109 E-4/B were also used several times successfully by Lehrgeschwader 2 in attacks on ships.

In the autumn of 1940, the E-7 version introduced not only the possibility of carrying additional tanks, and thus finally increasing the range, but also an aerodynamically revised propeller cover, since at least for the E series, after previous bad experiences, it was decided to dispense with a powered gun. When the German Wehrmacht sent troops to North Africa from February 1941, the fighter and fighter-bomber units assigned to the Afrika Korps were mainly equipped with Bf 109 E-4/Trop and E-7/Trop with sand filters. A few months later, during the attack on the Soviet Union, the Bf 109 E, whose time was slowly ticking away, once again proved its worth against all opponents. The last versions of the E series flew in operational units until late 1943, mainly as attack and reconnaissance aircraft.

Bf 109 E variants

- Bf 109 E-0: pre-production machine with DB-601-A-1 engine with 990 hp starting power; 4 × 7.92 mm MG 17 armament;
- Bf 109 E-1: fighter aircraft; engine and armament as E-0, but also possible DB 601 Aa with starting power of 1050 hp;
    - o Bf 109 E-1/B fighter-bomber; DB-601-Aa engine with 1050 hp starting power; Up to 250 kg bomb load;
- Bf 109 E-2: projected fighter aircraft; like E-1, but MG FF (motor gun) 20 mm; never built;
- Bf 109 E-3: fighter aircraft; Engines as E-1; Armament 2 × 7.92 mm MG 17, 2 × 20 mm MG FF in the wings;
    - o Bf 109 E-3a: export version; DB-601-Aa engine with 1050 hp starting power; Components declared as secret were not installed or replaced;
    - o Bf 109 E-3/B: fighter-bomber; engine and armament as E-3; bomb load up to 250 kg;
- Bf 109 E-4: fighter aircraft; engine as E-1, new cockpit cowling as standard; armament 2 × 7.92 mm MG 17, 2 × 20 mm MG FF/M in the wings;
    - o Bf 109 E-4/B: fighter-bomber; Engine as E-1/B; armament as E-4, bomb load up to 250 kg;
    - o Bf 109 E-4/N: fighter aircraft; as E-4, but DB 601 N engine with 1020 hp starting power, increased compression, C3 100 octane petrol;

▲ Bf 109A belonging to the Condor Legion with the insignia of Nationalist Spain.

▼ Bf 109E-4/Trop of JG 27 flies along the North African coast, summer 1941. Bundesarchiv. Author's colours.

▲ This insignia appeared in 1940 during the invasion of Norway, on a JG77 Bf 109T fighter. The Luftwaffe produced a great deal of creative design for the insignia of its units, which provided a strong esprit de corps among the pilots and ground crews. Bundesarchiv. Author colours.

MESSERSCHMITT BF 109 DIFFERENCES BETWEEN E7 AND T1 VERSION

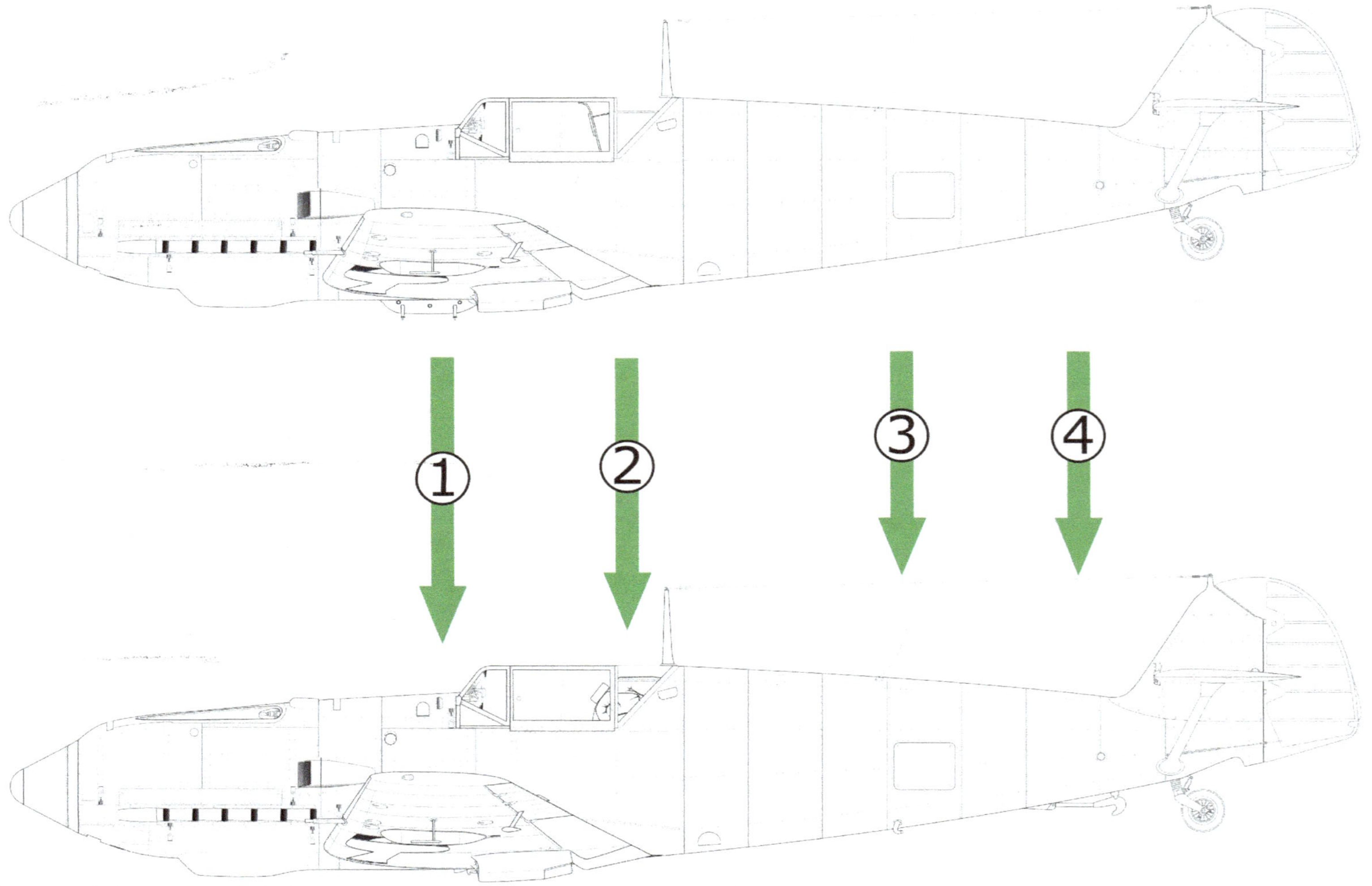

▲ Selected differences between BF 109 E7 and T1: 1. Extended wingspan (59 cm on each side) 2. Emergency equipment at sea (dinghy) and pilot's headrest for catapult take-off). 3. Accessories for catapult take-off under the wing root and panel number 5 of the fuselage.4. Stopping hook for landing the carrier.... Profiles by Björn Huber, licensed under CC BY-SA 3.0.

MESSERSCHMITT BF 109 E 3 III/ JG 54

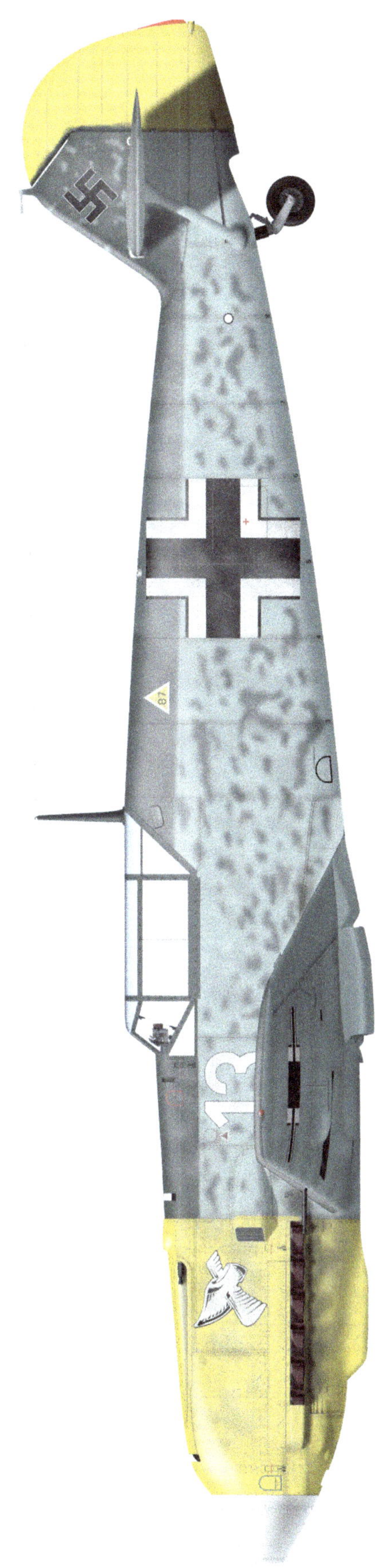

▲ Messerschmitt - Bf 109 E-3 of III./JG 54 (Jagdgeschwader 54) Battle of Britain, summer 1940. The emblem shows a Dutch sabot with wings, as the unit was based in the Netherlands at the time. Artwork by Björn Huber.

▲ Messerschmitt - Bf 109 E-4 of 9./JG 26 (Jagdgeschwader 26) from the Battle of Britain, summer 1940, flown by Oberleutnant Gerhard Schöpfel (45 air victories). Artwork by Björn Huber.

- o   Bf 109 E-4/BN: fighter-bomber; Engine and armament as E-4/N; Up to 250 kg bomb load;
- Bf 109 E-5: reconnaissance aircraft; based on E-3; Armament 2 × 7.92 mm MG 17; Camera RB 21/18 in the fuselage behind the cockpit;
- Bf 109 E-6: reconnaissance aircraft; based on E-4/N; armament 2 × 7.92 mm MG 17; hand-held camera RB 12.5/7.5 in the fuselage behind the cockpit;
- Bf 109 E-7: fighter and fighter-bomber; engine and armament as E-4; optional additional 300 l tank or bomb load up to 250 kg;
  - o   Bf 109 E-7/N: fighter and fighter-bomber; like E-7, but DB 601 N engine with 1020 hp starting power, increased compression, C3 100 octane petrol;
  - o   Bf 109 E-7/Z: high-altitude fighter, also E-7/NZ; like E-7/N, but with GM-1 injection for increased high-altitude performance;
  - o   Bf 109 E-7/U1: E-7 with armoured radiator;
  - o   Bf 109 E-7/U2: E-7 with armour against ground fire;
  - o   Bf 109 E-7/U3: reconnaissance aircraft, manual RB 12.5/7.5 camera in the fuselage behind the cockpit; RadioFuG17;
  - o   Bf 109 E-7/Trop: fighter and fighter-bomber; as E-7 with additional tropical equipment (sand filter, additional equipment);
- Bf 109 E-8: Fighter; Conversion from E-1 cells to accommodate additional 300-litre tanks;
- Bf 109 E-9: reconnaissance aircraft; based on E-7/N; Armament 2 × 7.92 mm MG 17; Camera RB-50/30.

▲ Several Luftwaffe Messerschmitt BF 109 E 3 by Jagdgeschwader-26. Bundesarchiv, author's colours.

▲ Bf-109E-3 of JG 51 'Mölders' at Deutsches Museum München. Wiki CC3 by Arjun Sarup

▼ A Messerschmitt Bf 109 E in the air force of Romania. Bundesarchiv, author colour.

EXPORT OF THE AIRCRAFT

In addition to the German air force (the Luftwaffe), this aircraft interested many other air forces that used the Fw fighter. It was mainly used by the Allies or neighbouring countries of the Third Reich, such as the Hungarian Air Force, Italy of the RSI, of course Spain and many others. A few were lost or captured by the Czechoslovaks, the British, the Americans and the Yugoslavs. Below is a brief summary of the models used of the BF 109 beyond the German borders.

COUNTRIES ALLIED OR FRIENDS OF GERMANY

Italy

The Bf 109 served in the ranks of both the Regia Aeronautica and the Aeronautica Nazionale Repubblicana. As early as 1937, the General Staff of the Blue Armed Forces had its eyes on this fantastic aircraft. Our pilots had to wait until 1943 before they were able to fly these machines (around 100 examples). Then came the armistice and supply ceased. It resumed later with the NRA, which at the end of the war received over 300 Model G machines.

Bulgarian Air Force

In 1940-1941 19 Me 109E-3 arrived to Bulgaria, in 1943 the first 23 Me 109G-2 fighter planes were delivered, altogether 46 G-2 and 99 G-6 served at the Bulgarian Air Force.

Hungarian Air Force

The Hungarian Air Force used a significant number of Me 109 fighters during the war, 3 D–1, 50 E–3, E–4, 66 F–4 and about 490 G–2, G–4, G–6, G–8, G–10, G–14.

Romanian Air Force

Had 50 E–3, –4, 19 E–7, 2 F–2, 5 F–4 and more than 235 G–2, G–4, G–6, G–8, 75 G–6a versions.

Slovakian Air Force

From 1942, the 13rd Fighter Squadron flew Me 109E, 12 (two E-2, one E-3, five E-4 and four E-7). The Fighter Squadron was deployed to the Eastern Front, between 1942-1943 flew E-4, F, and G-2,-4 version of the Me 109. For home defence against allied bombers G-6 were used. 16 E–3, 14 E–7 and 30 G–6

Japan

The governments of Germany and the Japanese Empire made arrangements to send two Bf 109Es to the Rising Sun as a first step towards licensed production of the aircraft at Kawasaki facilities. The aircraft arrived at their destination, but in fact production never started.

Spain

Ejército del Aire, some aircraft remained in Spanish ownership after the end of the Civil War. A post-World War II development by the Spanish led to the Hispano Aviación HA-1112 'Buchon', which remained on the line until the late 1950s if not beyond. The Hispano Aviation engineers combined the British Rolls Royce Merlin (engine of the Bf 109's great adversary, the Spitfire), with the basic airframe of the German machine, resulting in a far superior aircraft. It was used as a fighter and ground attack aircraft in various war campaigns in North Africa, with some success.

Croatian Air Force

More than 50 Me 109 served in the Air Force, E–4, F–2, G–2, G–6, G–10 and K versions.

Finnish Air Force

Finnish air forces were supplied with a good number of BF 109s. Used 162 Me 109 fighter planes, 48 G–2, 111 G–6 and 3 G–8

Yugoslavian Air Force

While the *Jugoslovensko kraljevsko ratno vazduhoplovstvo i pomorska avijacija* (Yugoslav Air Force), after months of negotiations, ordered fifty Bf 109E-3s from Germany in 1938, which was soon followed by another order for another fifty aircraft of the same type. Really Operated 73 Me 109E-3 fighter plane between 1939-1941.

GERMANY'S ENEMY OR NEUTRAL COUNTRIES

France

L'*Armée de l' air (Armée de l'air)*: at least one Bf 109E ended up in the hands of the French during the 1940 campaign against the Germans. The aircraft in question was forced to land in Amiens on 2 May 1940 due to technical problems and was immediately repainted in French Air Force colours. It was only used by one French pilot before being handed over to the RAF.

Great Britain

The *Royal Air Force* had at its disposal at least four Bf 109s that fell into British hands: the Bf 109E given up by the French, another Bf 109E-1 and two Bf 109E-4s. The example acquired by the French Air Force was transferred to the base at Boscombe Down and, like the other three Bf 109s, served on numerous missions with RAF squadrons.

Soviet Union

The Russian Air Force (*Voenno-vozdušnye sily*) had five 'Emil' aircraft sent from Germany before the start of hostilities in 1939-1940.

Sweden

The *Svenska Flygvapnet* also had its Bf; it all happened on 24 October 1940: a Bf 109E-1 from the 4th squadron of JG 77 was forced to land on Swedish soil due to technical problems. The German pilot was interned but the aircraft was probably painted in Swedish Air Force colours and actually used in flight. The aircraft was later the subject of a diplomatic exchange in November 1940.

Switzerland

Switzerland was the first foreign country to purchase Messerschmitt fighters. Between December 1938 and mid-January 1939, the Swiss country received its first ten Bf 109D-2s, designated J-301 to J-310. These were used as training aircraft by Fliegerkompanie (flight companies) numbers 6, 15 and 21 based in Thun, Payerne and Dübendorf respectively. A consignment of a further eighty Bf 109 E-3s was delivered to Switzerland between April 1939 and April 1940, which thus became the largest foreign buyer of the Bf 109E.

POST-WAR PRODUCTION

Israel

Heyl Ha'Avir: After the war, Israel employed a model derived from the Bf 109, the Czech Avia S-199 during the 1948 war.

MESSERSCHMITT BF 109 E 4 JG 27 WERNER SCHROER

▲ Messerschmitt - BBf 109 E-4/Trop of I./JG 27 (Jagdgeschwader 27) North Africa 1941, flown by Leutnant Werner Schroer (114 air victories). Artwork by Björn Huber.

MESSERSCHMITT BF 109 E 7 B 8/ZG 1

▲ Messerschmitt -Bf 109 E-7B of 8./ZG 1 (Zerstörergeschwader 1) Russia 1941. After the adoption of the Bf 109 F by the fighter units of the Luftwaffe, many E versions were assigned to fighter-bomber and destroyer units.
The ZG 1 was also known as the 'Wespen-Geschwader' (Wasp Squadron). Artwork by Björn Huber.

MESSERSCHMITT BF 109 E 4 B III/ JG 1

▲ Messerschmitt - Bf 109 E-4B of III./JG 1 (Jagdgeschwader 1) Netherlands, spring 1942. After the Battle of Britain, several Jagdgeschwader formed Jabo (Jagdbomber - fighter-bomber) units to attack targets on the British coast. Artwork by Björn Huber.

▲ A Messerschmitt Bf 109 E3 in flight. Bundesarchiv.

▼ Preparation for the flight of a BF-109 at an occupied French airport. Bundesarchiv, author colour.

DATASHEET B-C-D-E SERIES

Parameter	Data
MESSERSCHMITT BF 109 B1 1936	
Crew	1
Length	8,55 m
Wingspan	9,87 m
Height	2,60 m
Wing surface area	16,2 m^2
Initial mass	2.200 kg (excluding armament)
Wing loading	136 kg/mq
Engine	Junkers Jumo 210D with 12-cylinder V-engine with maximum starting power of 680 hp
Maximum speed	470 km/h at an altitude of 4,000 m
Climb speed	approximately 17m per second
Peak height	9.000 m
Fuel	400 litres
Armament	two 7.92 mm MG 17s (500 rounds each) above the engine, firing synchronously through the propeller circuit. Initially one MG 17 behind the engine block (non-synchronised, firing in the hollow shaft of the propeller).

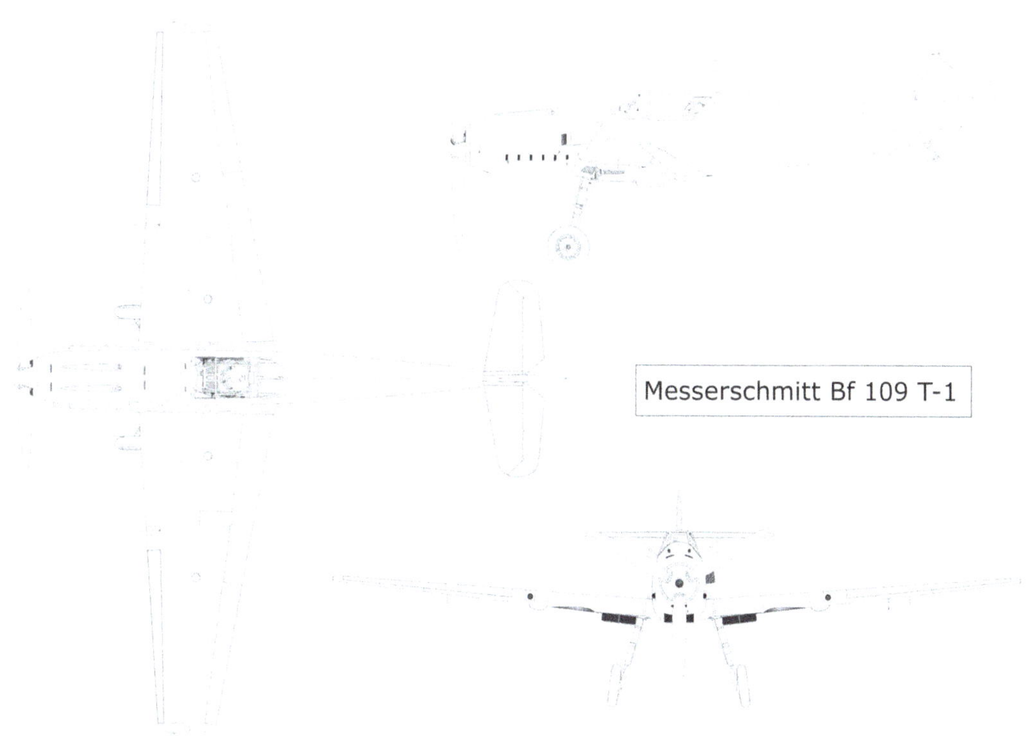

▲ Diagram of the Messerschmitt BF 109 T-1. Work by Bjorn Huber, licensed under CC BY-SA 3.0.

MESSERSCHMITT BF 109 C1 1937	
Parameter	**Data**
Length	8,55 m
Wingspan	9,87 m
Height	2,60 m
Wing surface area	16,2 m^2
Initial mass	2.310 kg (excluding armament)
Engine	Junkers Jumo 210 G 12-cylinder with maximum starting power of 700 hp
Maximum speed	440 km/h at an altitude of 4,000 m
Climb speed	approximately 17m per second
Peak height	9.500 m
Fuel	400 litres
Armament	Four MG 17 7.92 mm, two of which were above the engine (500 rounds each), firing synchronously through the propeller circuit, and two unsynchronised in the wings (420 rounds each).

MESSERSCHMITT BF 109 D1 WITH JUMO 1937	
Parameter	**Data**
Length	8,64 m
Wingspan	9,87 m
Height	2,60 m
Wing surface area	16,2 m^2
Initial mass	2.170 kg (excluding armament)
Engine	Junkers Jumo 210 D with 12 cylinders and a maximum starting power of 680 hp
Maximum speed	460 km/h at an altitude of 4,000 m
Climb speed	approximately 18m per second
Peak height	9.500 m
Autonomy	400 litres
Armament	four 7.92 mm MG 17s, two of which were above the engine (500 rounds each), firing synchronously through the propeller circuit and two unsynchronised in the wings (420 rounds each).

MESSERSCHMITT BF 109 E3 1939	
Parameter	**Data**
Length	8.64 m
Wingspan	9,87 m
Height	2,60 m
Wing surface area	16,2 m^2
Initial mass	2.505 kg (excluding armament)
Engine	12-cylinder Daimler-Benz DB 601 A-1 V-engine with 990 hp PAM
Maximum speed	570 km/h at an altitude of 5,000 m
Climb speed	approximately 18m per second
Peak height	10.500 m
Autonomy	400 litres
Armament	two 7.92 mm MG 17s above the engine (1000 rounds each) and two 20 mm MG FF automatic cannons in the wings, firing outside the propeller circle (60 rounds each).

BIBLIOGRAPHY

- Walter J. Boyne, *Scontro di ali: l'aviazione militare nella Seconda guerra mondiale*, Milano, Mursia, 1997, ISBN 88-425-2256-2.
- William Green, Gordon Swanborough, *The Great Book of Fighters*, St. Paul, Minnesota, MBI Publishing, 2001, ISBN 0-7603-1194-3.
- Robert Jackson, *The forgotten Aces – The story of the unsung Heroes of Worls War II*, London, Sphere Books Limited, 1989, ISBN 0-7474-0310-4.
- Robert Jackson, *Messerschmitt Bf 109 A-D Series* (Air Vanguard 18), Osprey Publishing, 2015, ISBN 978-1-4728-0487-7.
- Francis K. Mason, *Messerschmitt Bf 109 B,C,D,E in Luftwaffe & foreign service, Aircam aviation series n° 39*, vol. I, Osprey Publishing, ISBN 0-85045-152-3.
- Giovanni Massimello, Giorgio Apostolo, *Italian Aces of World War 2*, Osprey Publishing, 2000, ISBN 1-84176-078-1.
- David Mondey, *The Hamlyn Concise Guide to Axis Aircraft of World War II*, Londra, Bounty Books, 2006, ISBN 0-7537-1460-4.
- Hans Werner Neulen, *In the Skies of Europe*, Marlborough, The Crowood Press, 2000, ISBN 1-86126-799-1.
- Giuseppe Pesce, Giovanni Massimello, *Adriano Visconti - Asso di guerra*, Parma, Albertelli Edizioni, 1997, ISBN non esistente.
- Mike Spick, *The complete Fighter Ace All the World's Fighter Aces, 1914-2000*, Londra, Greenhill Books, 1999.
- Ulrich Steinhilper, Peter Osborne, *Spitfire on my tail: A view from the other side*, Bromley, Independent Books, 2006, ISBN 1-872836-00-3.
- AAVV, *War Machines*, Osprey Publishing, Londra 1984
- Gordon Williamson, *Aces of the Reich*, Arms and Armour, Londra 1988
- Caldwell, Donald L. *JG 26: Top Guns of the Luftwaffe*. New York: Ballantine Books, 1991. ISBN 0-8041-1050-6
- Cross, Roy and Gerald Scarborough. *Messerschmitt Bf 109, Versions B-E*. London: Patrick Stevens, 1976. ISBN 0-85059-106-6
- Feist, Uwe. *The Fighting Me 109*. London: Arms and Armour Press, 1993, ISBN 1-85409-209-X.
- Green, William. *Messerschmitt Bf 109: The Augsburg Eagle; A Documentary History*. London: Macdonald and Jane's Publishing Group Ltd., 1980. ISBN 0-7106-0005-4
- Griehl, Manfred. *Das geheime Typenbuch der deutschen Luftwaffe: Geheime Kommandosache 8531/44 gKdos* (in German). Friedberg, Germany: Podzun-Pallas Verlag, 2004. ISBN 978-3-7909-0775-9
- Kaplan, Philip: *Fighter Aces of the Luftwaffe in World War II*, 2007 Pen & Sword Aviation Publ., Auldgirth, ISBN 978-1-84415-460-9.
- John Weal, *Jagdgeschwader 52 The Experten* (Aviation Elite), Oxford, Osprey Publishing Ltd, 2004, ISBN 978-1-84176-786-4.
- Ritger, Lynn. *Meserschmitt Bf 109 Prototype to 'E' Variants*. Bedford, UK: SAM Publications, 2006. ISBN 978-0-9551858-0-9.
- Martin Caidin: *Die Me109. (US-Originaltitel: Me109)* Verlag Arthur Moewig, 1968, 192 Seiten (dt.: 1981), ISBN 3-8118-4369-9.
- Willy Radinger, Walter Schick, Wolfgang Otto: *Messerschmitt Me 109. Alle Varianten von Bf (Me) 109A bis K*. Aviatic, Oberhaching 2011, ISBN 978-3-925505-93-5.

- Peter Schmoll: *Messerschmitt Me 109. Produktion und Einsatz*. MZ-Buchverlag, Regenstauf 2017, ISBN 978-3-86646-356-1.
- Ralf Swoboda, Hans-Jürgen Becker: *Flugzeuge und Hubschrauber der Luftwaffe, des Heeres und der Kriegsmarine : 1933–1945*. Motorbuch Verlag, Stuttgart 2005, ISBN 3-613-02524-8.
- Kyrill v. Gersdorff, Helmut Schubert, Stefan Ebert: *Flugmotoren und Strahltriebwerke*. Bernard & Graefe Verlag, Bonn 2007, ISBN 978-3-7637-6128-9.
- Ernst König: *Die Geschichte der Luftwaffe*. Rastatt 1980.
- Rüdiger Kosin: *Die Entwicklung der deutschen Jagdflugzeuge*. Bernard & Graefe Verlag, 1990.
- Heinz J. Nowarra: *Die deutsche Luftrüstung 1933–1945. Band 3*, Bernard & Graefe Verlag, 1993.
- Hans Redemann: *Die bahnbrechenden Konstruktionen im Flugzeugbau*. Motorbuch Verlag, Stuttgart 1989, ISBN 3-613-01293-6.
- Walter Schuck: *Abschuss. Von der Me 109 zur Me 262*. Helios-Verlag, Aachen 2008, 2. Auflage, ISBN 978-3-938208-44-1.
- Jochen Prien, Gerhard Stemmer, Peter Rodeike, Winfried Bock: *Die Jagdfliegerverbände der Deutschen Luftwaffe 1934 bis 1945. Teil 1*, struve Verlag, 2000.
- Jochen Prien, Peter Rodeicke: *Messerschmitt Bf 109 F, G & K Series. 2. Auflage*. Schiffer books, 1995.
- John R. Beaman, Jerry L. Campbell: *Messerschmitt Bf 109 in action (Part 1)*. Squadron/Signal Publications, 1980.
- John R. Beaman, Jerry L. Campbell: *Messerschmitt Bf 109 in action (Part 2)*. Squadron/Signal Publications, 1980.
- William Green: *War planes of the Second World War. Vol. 1–4 und 8–10* / Macdonald & Co Ltd. London 1960–1968.
- Aleš Janda, Tomáš Poruba: *Messerschmitt Bf 109 of JG 52 in Deutsch Brod*. JaPo Verlag, 2007.

▲ A perfectly preserved Messerschmitt Bf 109E4 during an aviation exhibition.

TWE-018 EN